EXPLORE OUTER SPACE

THE MOON

by Ruth Owen

WINDMILL BOOKS
NEW YORK

Published in 2014 by Windmill Books, An Imprint of Rosen Publishing
29 East 21st Street, New York, NY 10010

Produced for Windmill by Ruby Tuesday Books Ltd
Editor for Ruby Tuesday Books Ltd: Mark J. Sachner
US Editor: Sara Howell
Designer: Emma Randall
Consultant: Kevin Yates, Fellow of the Royal Astronomical Society

Photo Credits:
Cover, 1, 4–5, 10–11, 13 (top), 20–21, 22–23 © Shutterstock; 6–7, 9, 19, 23 (right) © Ruby Tuesday Books Ltd; 13 (bottom) © Public domain; 15, 16–17, 25 (bottom), 27, 28–29 © NASA; 25 (top) © Science Photo Library.

Library of Congress Cataloging-in-Publication Data

Owen, Ruth, 1967–
The moon / by Ruth Owen.
    p. cm. — (Explore outer space)
Includes index.
ISBN 978-1-61533-721-7 (library binding) — ISBN 978-1-61533-759-0 (pbk.) —
ISBN 978-1-61533-760-6 (6-pack)
1. Moon—Juvenile literature. 2. Moon—Exploration—Juvenile literature. I. Title. II. Series: Owen, Ruth, 1967– Explore outer space.
QB582.O94 2014
523.3—dc23
                                2013002228

Manufactured in the United States of America

CPSIA Compliance Information: Batch #B3S13WM: For Further Information contact Windmill Books, New York, New York at 1-866-478-0556

CONTENTS

OUR MOON

Traveling through space at an average distance of about 238,855 miles (384,400 km) from Earth is the Moon. This rocky ball has been our planet's constant companion for about 4.5 billion years.

A **moon** is a naturally occurring **satellite** that **orbits** a **planet**. Earth's moon is simply called the Moon because until the Italian **astronomer** Galileo Galilei discovered four of Jupiter's many moons in 1610, people believed that Earth's moon was the only one in existence.

Today, we know of over 170 moons orbiting planets in the **solar system**. Some planets have many moons. Others, like Earth, have just one. These other moons may have been given more glamorous names, such as Titan, Ferdinand, Cressida, and Miranda. Our plain old Moon, however, has one very important claim to fame. Its rocky, dusty surface is the only place in the **universe** other than Earth where a human has ever stood.

This image shows just some of the views we see of the Moon from Earth.

The Moon is traveling through space at nearly 2,300 miles per hour (3,700 km/h).

That's Out of This World!

When you gaze at the Moon, it looks as if it is shining with a bright white, yellow, or bluish-white light. The Moon has no light of its own, though. It looks bright because it reflects light from the Sun, just as a mirror reflects the bright light given off by a light bulb.

IN PERFECT HARMONY

As our planet Earth orbits the Sun, our little companion, the Moon, is orbiting Earth.

The Moon makes one complete orbit of Earth every 27.3 days. As it orbits, it follows an elliptical, or slightly oval, path. This means that sometimes the Moon is closer to Earth, and sometimes it is farther away. These two points are called the **perigee** (when the Moon is closest to Earth) and the **apogee** (when it is farthest away).

Earth spins on its **axis** and makes one complete rotation every 24 hours. As Earth spins, the half of the planet facing the Sun experiences daytime, while the half facing away experiences night. The Moon acts in this way, too. The Moon, however, rotates much slower than Earth. It takes about 27.3 days to make one rotation. This means that a day on the Moon lasts for about two weeks. Then it is night for two weeks.

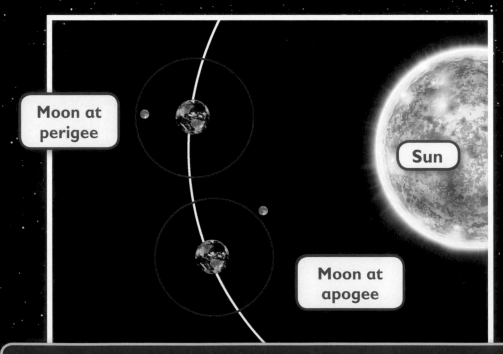

This diagram shows how Earth orbits the Sun (the white line), while the Moon orbits Earth (the red line). The diagram is not to scale.

That's Out of This World!

Even though the Moon is spinning on its axis, we always see the same side of the Moon from Earth. This is because the time it takes the Moon to make one full rotation is almost the same as the time it takes to orbit Earth once. These timings mean that the same part of the Moon is always pointing toward Earth (see diagrams below).

This diagram shows how the Moon rotates counterclockwise on its own axis over 27.3 days. If seen from above, the red portion of the Moon in this diagram is the surface facing toward Earth.

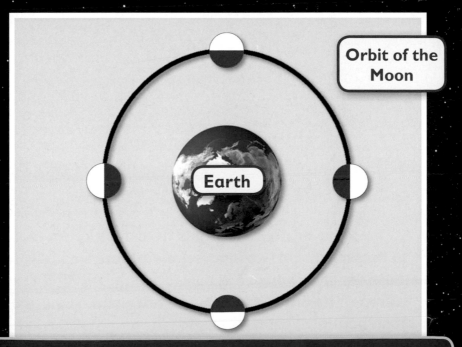

Orbit of the Moon

Earth

In this diagram, you can see how the Moon's rotation, in conjunction with its orbit of Earth, means we always see the same part of the Moon from Earth.

THE PHASES OF THE MOON

Sometimes the Moon appears in the sky as a thin crescent shape. At other times it looks like a giant white disk, which is known as a **full moon**. These changing views of the Moon in the night sky are known as phases.

We see the Moon go through different phases because as it orbits Earth, different parts of the Moon catch the Sun's light. You can see how this happens in the diagram to the right. It shows the Moon making one orbit of Earth. The inner ring of small Moons in the diagram shows how the Sun's light hits the Moon's surface. The outer ring of larger Moons shows what we see from here on Earth.

When we see a full moon, the Moon is on the opposite side of the Earth to the Sun. The whole surface of the Moon is lit up by the Sun's light, so the Moon appears as a shining white disk.

That's Out of This World!

As the Moon orbits, it changes from a dark new moon to become a thin waxing, or growing, crescent. More and more of its surface becomes visible until, halfway through its orbit, it becomes a full moon. Then, the Moon begins to wane, or disappear again. The waxing and waning gibbous phases get their name because the word "gibbous" means "humped."

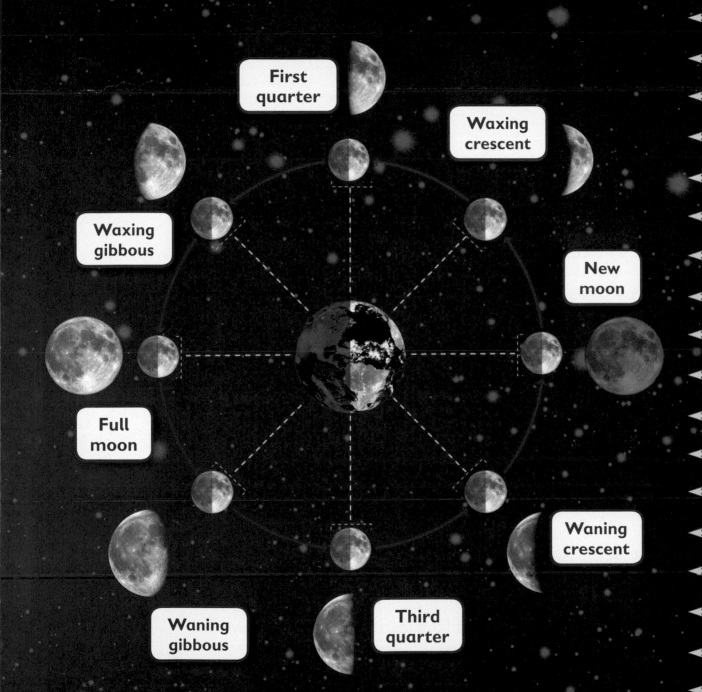

This diagram shows the Moon's phases during one orbit of Earth.

First quarter

Waxing crescent

Waxing gibbous

New moon

Full moon

Waning crescent

Waning gibbous

Third quarter

LIGHT FROM THE SUN

THE BIRTH OF THE MOON

Every object in the solar system, including Earth and the Moon, is orbiting the Sun.

The Sun formed about 4.5 billion years ago when gas and dust in a vast space cloud began to collapse on itself, forming a massive, rotating sphere, or ball. The material in the sphere was pressed together by **gravity**, causing pressure and enormous heat to build. Finally, the sphere ignited, and the Sun was born!

Leftover matter from the formation of the Sun clumped together to form the planets and other objects in the solar system. Then, when the Earth was about 4.5 billion years old, its Moon was born.

Over the years there have been many theories as to how the Moon formed. Today, most scientists believe a planet, or some other space body, the size of Mars crashed into the young Earth. Superheated chunks of Earth and the impactor planet flew out into space. Over time this debris clumped together to form the Moon, which has continued to orbit Earth to this day.

That's Out of This World!

Past theories of how the Moon came to be Earth's space partner include the idea that the Moon formed alongside the Earth from material left over from the birth of the Sun. Another theory was that the Moon formed far from Earth. When the orbits of the two objects crossed, Earth's gravity captured the Moon, pulling the smaller object into a new orbit.

This illustration shows how the Moon may have been formed.

Earth

Mars-sized body

THE MOON, INSIDE AND OUT

The Moon looks round, but it is actually shaped more like an egg. Scientists believe that, like Earth, the Moon is made up of different layers.

Deep within the Moon's center is an inner core of solid iron. This inner core is surrounded by an outer core of **molten**, liquid iron enclosed within a boundary layer of partially melted iron. Surrounding the core is a partially molten rocky layer called the mantle. The Moon's outer layer is a rocky crust with an average depth of 50 miles (80 km).

Beyond the Moon's surface, there is nothing! Unlike Earth, which is surrounded by a layer of gases, the Moon has no **atmosphere**. This means there is no air on the Moon.

The Moon's lack of atmosphere means there are no protective gases to shield its surface from the Sun's heat by day or to trap heat that can warm the surface at night. In the day, temperatures may reach 253°F (123°C). At night, temperatures can plummet to −387°F (−233°C).

That's Out of This World!

The Moon has one-sixth of the gravity of Earth. So, if you weigh 120 pounds (54 kg) on Earth, you will only weigh 20 pounds (9 kg) on the Moon. Having low gravity makes walking easier. So on the Moon, a person could bounce from step to step.

The Moon
Radius = 1,080 miles
(1,738 km)

Earth
Radius = 3,959 miles
(6,371 km)

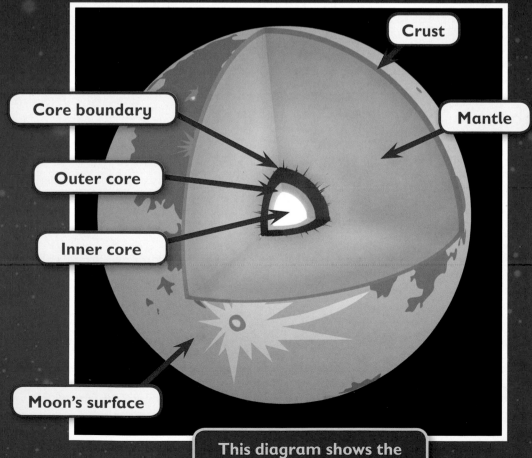

Crust

Core boundary

Mantle

Outer core

Inner core

Moon's surface

This diagram shows the
internal layers of the Moon.

THE SURFACE OF THE MOON

When there's a bright, white full Moon in the sky, it's fascinating to look up at our closest space neighbor and see the areas of light and dark on its surface. With telescopes and other imaging equipment, it's possible to see the landscape of the Moon in beautiful detail.

The dark areas on the Moon's surface are called *mare*, which is the Latin word for sea. They got their name because hundreds of years ago, the astronomer Galileo thought these dark areas were seas. Today we know they are basins on the Moon's surface that are filled with a type of rock called basalt.

Basalt is **lava** that has cooled and hardened. Billions of years ago, parts of the Moon's mantle were superheated and molten. The liquid rock, or lava, rose to the surface and burst through cracks in the Moon's crust in just the same way that lava erupts from volcanoes on Earth. Today, there are no active volcanoes on The Moon. Now there are just vast solid plains of basalt rock.

That's Out of This World!

The paler areas on the Moon's surface are known as *terrae*, or highlands. There are even mountains on the Moon reaching heights of up to 16,000 feet (5,000 m).

Mountain range

Mare

Craters

Terrae, or highlands

This image shows surface details of the Moon's near side, which is the side we can always see from Earth.

CRATERS ON THE MOON

The Moon's lack of an atmosphere has helped shape its surface. Over the billions of years of the Moon's lifetime, hundreds of thousands of **asteroids**, **meteoroids**, and other space bodies have crashed into the Moon.

These impacts happen because the Moon has no atmosphere to cause the space debris to burn up. The impacts have left the Moon's surface scarred by deep craters.

Scientists have estimated that there are around 300,000 craters of nearly 1 mile (1.6 km) in diameter, just on the Moon's near side. Many impact craters are hundreds of miles (km) in diameter and thousands of feet (m) deep!

All these impacts have also smashed and broken up the upper layer of the Moon's crust. The Moon's surface is covered by a deep layer of broken rock called **regolith**. The regolith varies in size from tiny dust-sized particles to huge boulders the size of trucks.

Craters

South Pole-Aitken basin

This image shows the many craters at the Moon's South Pole.

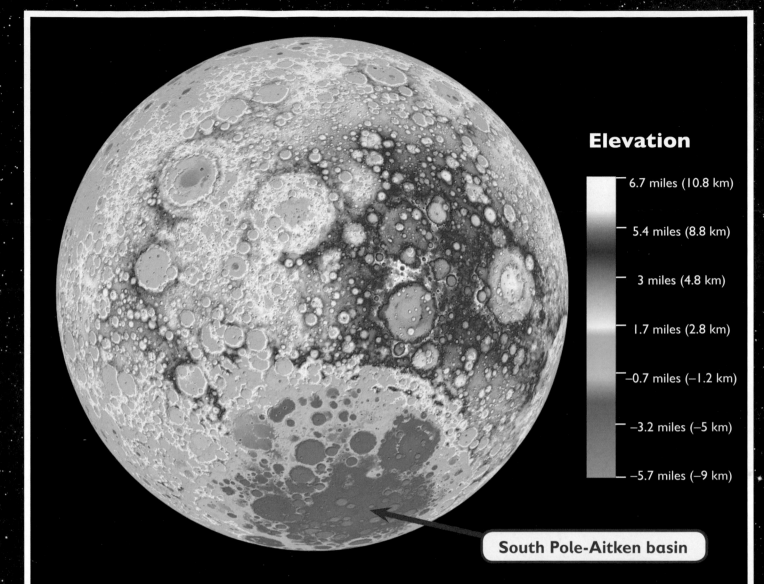

Elevation

6.7 miles (10.8 km)	
5.4 miles (8.8 km)	
3 miles (4.8 km)	
1.7 miles (2.8 km)	
−0.7 miles (−1.2 km)	
−3.2 miles (−5 km)	
−5.7 miles (−9 km)	

South Pole-Aitken basin

This image shows the topography (physical features) of the far side of the Moon.

That's Out of This World!

The largest impact crater, or basin, on the Moon's surface is the South Pole-Aitken basin. It has a diameter of 1,600 miles (2,600 km) and is more than 5 miles (8 km) deep.

LUNAR ECLIPSES

An exciting phenomena that everyone can see from Earth without the need for a telescope or special equipment is called a lunar eclipse.

As Earth moves around the Sun, it casts two shadows, called the penumbral shadow and the umbral shadow. Sometimes, when the moon is in its full moon phase, it passes through these shadows (see diagram 1).

The Moon doesn't pass through the shadows on every orbit. Most of the time, the Moon orbits above or below the shadows cast by Earth because its path is slightly tilted (see diagram 2). Sometimes, however, the Moon's orbit takes it through Earth's shadow. This is when a lunar eclipse happens.

As a section of the Moon passes through Earth's umbral shadow, we see that area of the Moon become dark. This is called a partial lunar eclipse (see diagram 3).

That's Out of This World!

The word lunar comes from the Latin word "luna," which means "moon."

Diagram 1

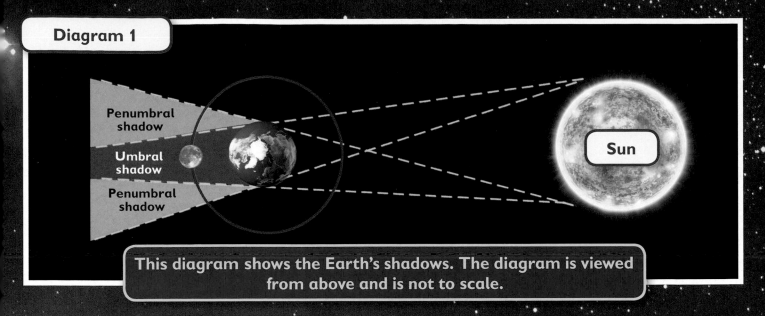

Penumbral shadow

Umbral shadow

Penumbral shadow

Sun

This diagram shows the Earth's shadows. The diagram is viewed from above and is not to scale.

Diagram 2

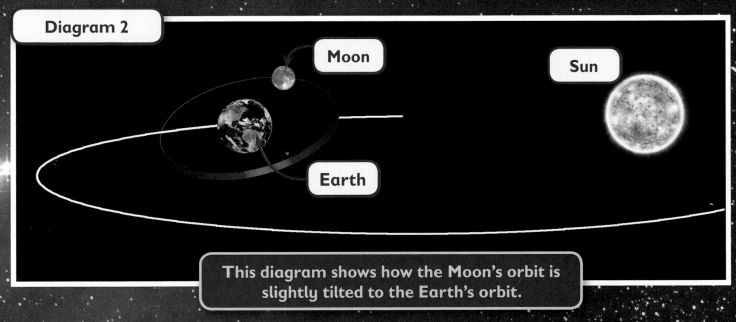

Moon

Sun

Earth

This diagram shows how the Moon's orbit is slightly tilted to the Earth's orbit.

Diagram 3

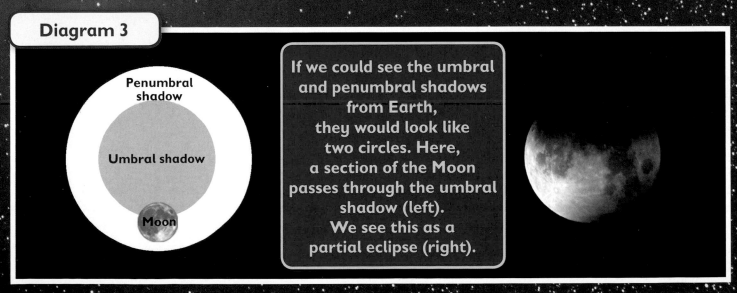

Penumbral shadow

Umbral shadow

Moon

If we could see the umbral and penumbral shadows from Earth, they would look like two circles. Here, a section of the Moon passes through the umbral shadow (left). We see this as a partial eclipse (right).

THE MOON AND TIDES

If you've ever spent a day at the beach, you have seen how the ocean's water level rises and falls. This change in water levels, called the tide, is actually caused by the Moon.

The Moon's gravity pulls things on Earth toward it. Solid things, such as mountains, only move the tiniest amount, so it's not noticeable. Water, however, moves easily.

On the side of the Earth closest to the Moon, the Moon's gravity pulls at the oceans, causing the water to bulge (see diagram 1, point A). A second bulge also happens on the opposite side of the Earth (point C) because the Moon is pulling the Earth away from the water on that side. On Earth, these two bulges of water are experienced as high tides. The water level rises by several feet (m), filling up harbors and coves and pushing the ocean further up the beach. As points A and C experience a high tide, points B and D have a low tide, during which the water level drops.

As the Earth rotates in relation to the Moon once every 24 hours, each place on Earth takes its turn to be in position A, B, C, and D. So every place experiences two high tides and two low tides every 24 hours.

That's Out of This World!

The Sun is a long way from Earth, but its gravitational pull also affects the Earth's tides. When the Sun and Moon are in line (see diagram 2), they both pull on the oceans, making the water bulges larger. When the Moon, Earth, and Sun form a right angle (see diagram 3), the Sun counteracts the Moon's gravity, making the bulges smaller.

Diagram 1

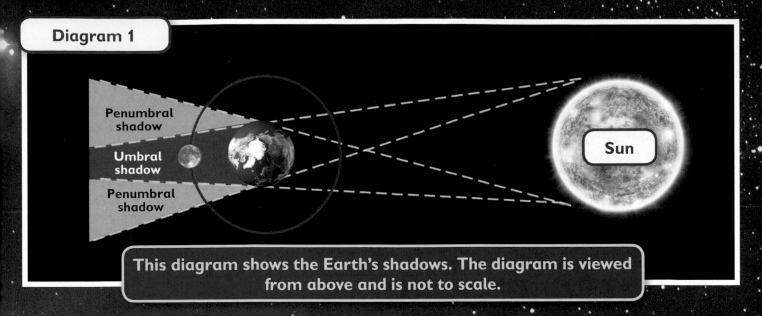

Penumbral shadow

Umbral shadow

Penumbral shadow

Sun

This diagram shows the Earth's shadows. The diagram is viewed from above and is not to scale.

Diagram 2

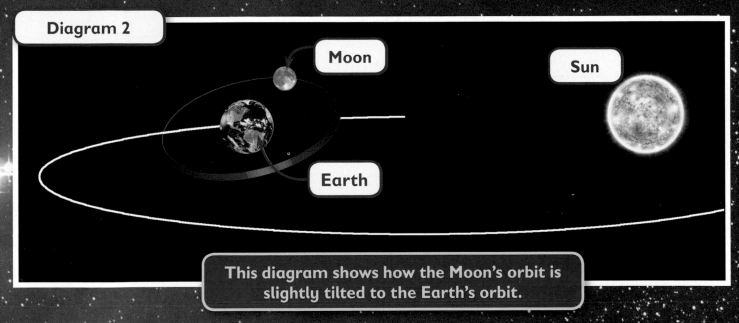

Moon

Sun

Earth

This diagram shows how the Moon's orbit is slightly tilted to the Earth's orbit.

Diagram 3

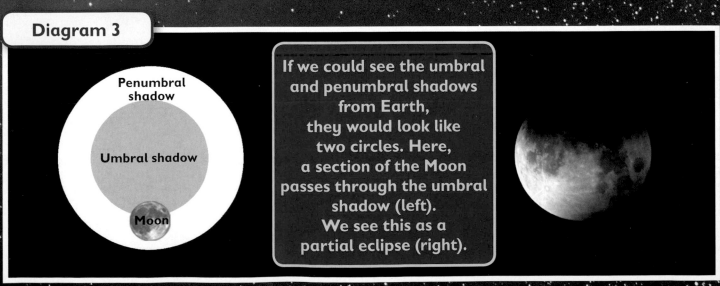

Penumbral shadow

Umbral shadow

Moon

If we could see the umbral and penumbral shadows from Earth, they would look like two circles. Here, a section of the Moon passes through the umbral shadow (left). We see this as a partial eclipse (right).

TOTAL LUNAR ECLIPSES

It's possible to see a lunar eclipse from somewhere on Earth about two to four times a year.

Sometimes the orbit of the Moon is just right for the entire Moon to pass through Earth's umbral shadow. Then, a total lunar eclipse occurs. You might expect that the whole face of the Moon would turn dark during a total eclipse. In fact, the Moon becomes a reddish-orange color.

As the Sun's light passes around Earth, Earth's atmosphere bends the light. This enables some of the light to reach the Moon and illuminate it. The Sun's light is made up of many colors. Earth's atmosphere only lets through red or orange light, however, so that is why the Moon is lit up in reds and oranges. If Earth had no atmosphere, the Moon would appear completely black during a total lunar eclipse.

The stages of a total lunar eclipse

That's Out of This World!

The Moon is slowly drifting away from Earth.
Every year it moves about 1.6 inches (4 cm)
away from our planet.

The Moon and Tides

If you've ever spent a day at the beach, you have seen how the ocean's water level rises and falls. This change in water levels, called the tide, is actually caused by the Moon.

The Moon's gravity pulls things on Earth toward it. Solid things, such as mountains, only move the tiniest amount, so it's not noticeable. Water, however, moves easily.

On the side of the Earth closest to the Moon, the Moon's gravity pulls at the oceans, causing the water to bulge (see diagram 1, point A). A second bulge also happens on the opposite side of the Earth (point C) because the Moon is pulling the Earth away from the water on that side. On Earth, these two bulges of water are experienced as high tides. The water level rises by several feet (m), filling up harbors and coves and pushing the ocean further up the beach. As points A and C experience a high tide, points B and D have a low tide, during which the water level drops.

As the Earth rotates in relation to the Moon once every 24 hours, each place on Earth takes its turn to be in position A, B, C, and D. So every place experiences two high tides and two low tides every 24 hours.

That's Out of This World!

The Sun is a long way from Earth, but its gravitational pull also affects the Earth's tides. When the Sun and Moon are in line (see diagram 2), they both pull on the oceans, making the water bulges larger. When the Moon, Earth, and Sun form a right angle (see diagram 3), the Sun counteracts the Moon's gravity, making the bulges smaller.

22

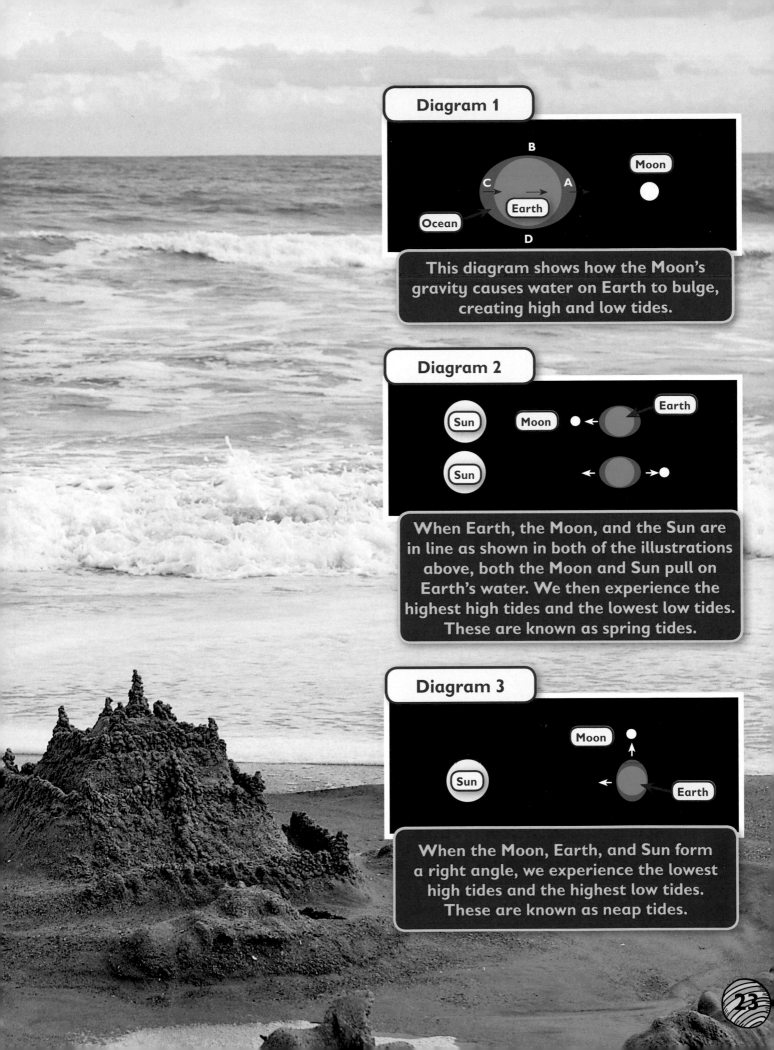

Diagram 1

B

C → Earth → A

Ocean →

D

Moon

This diagram shows how the Moon's gravity causes water on Earth to bulge, creating high and low tides.

Diagram 2

Sun   Moon ● ← Earth

Sun   ← ● →

When Earth, the Moon, and the Sun are in line as shown in both of the illustrations above, both the Moon and Sun pull on Earth's water. We then experience the highest high tides and the lowest low tides. These are known as spring tides.

Diagram 3

Moon ●

Sun   ← ● Earth

When the Moon, Earth, and Sun form a right angle, we experience the lowest high tides and the highest low tides. These are known as neap tides.

THE RACE IS ON!

For centuries, the best way for people to study the Moon was by looking at it through telescopes. All that changed as a result of the space race. This was a competition that started in the 1950s between the United States and the former **Soviet Union**.

Some of the most exciting events that took place during the space race involved exploring the Moon. In 1959, an unmanned Soviet Luna mission landed the first spacecraft, called *Luna 2*, on the surface of the Moon. Later that year, *Luna 3* did a lunar flyby, sending back photographs of the far side of the Moon. The far side is always facing away from Earth.

Viewing this half of our nearest **extraterrestrial** neighbor, a side that humans had never before seen, was an awe-inspiring event. But the biggest prize in the space race was yet to come. In 1969, the Apollo 11 mission would send a crew of US **astronauts** to the Moon, land them safely, and return them to Earth.

That's Out of This World!

The space race was a competition to become the dominant nation in space exploration. In 1957, the Soviet Union launched the first artificial satellite to orbit Earth. In 1961, the Soviets scored another victory, sending a spacecraft containing the first human, a Russian **cosmonaut**, into Earth's orbit. Each of these "firsts" was quickly followed by a similar exploit by the United States. The space race was definitely on!

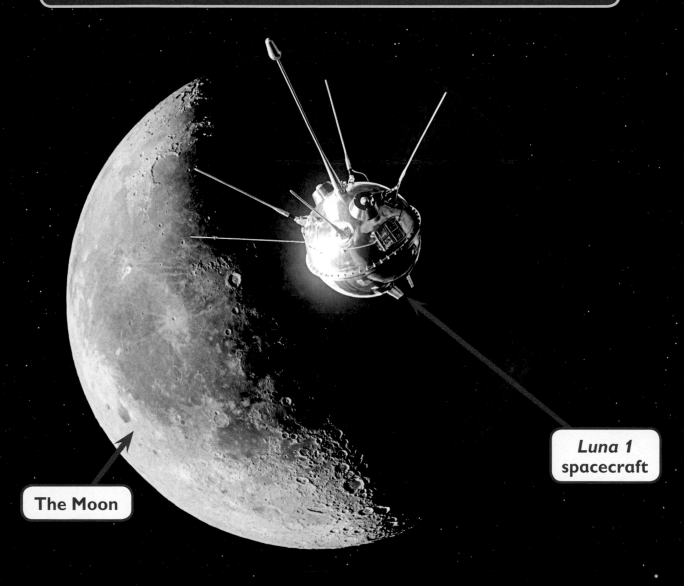

This artwork shows the Soviet Union's *Luna 1*, which was the first spacecraft to leave the Earth's atmosphere. It was designed to impact the Moon, but it missed and went into orbit around the Sun.

The Moon

***Luna 1* spacecraft**

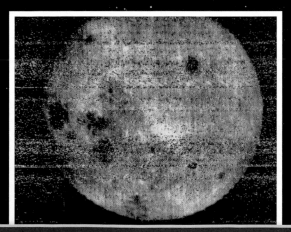

The *Luna 3* spacecraft sent the image (left) of the far side of the Moon back to Earth in 1959. Fifty years later, NASA's Lunar Reconnaissance Orbiter captured the image (right) of the Moon's far side.

APOLLO 11: FOOTPRINTS ON THE MOON

July 20, 1969, 4:18 p.m., Eastern Daylight Time. The event was the touchdown by *Eagle*, the US Apollo **11 lunar module**, onto the surface of the Moon. This historical moment is the first landing of humans on another world.

Six hours later, with billions of their fellow Earthlings watching on TV, Neil Armstrong and then Buzz Aldrin became the first humans to set foot on the Moon. They stayed on the lunar surface for two hours 36 minutes before returning to the *Eagle*. There, they prepared to blast off to rejoin the third Apollo 11 astronaut, Michael Collins, who was orbiting above the Moon in the **command module**, *Columbia*. All three then rocketed back to Earth.

Eight years earlier, in May 1961, only weeks after the first human had been launched into space, US president John F. Kennedy boldly set forth the following national goal: "… before this decade is out, of landing a man on the Moon and returning him safely to the Earth." Tragically, Kennedy's life was ended by an assassin's bullet in 1963. In 1969, however, his promise was fulfilled by the Apollo 11 Moon landing.

That's Out of This World!

With the Apollo 11 Moon landing, the space race between the United States and the Soviet Union was for the most part over. The Soviets did not make any manned flights to the Moon, but five more Apollo missions landed American astronauts on the Moon. The missions, which ended in 1972, allowed a total of 12 astronauts to actually walk on the lunar surface.

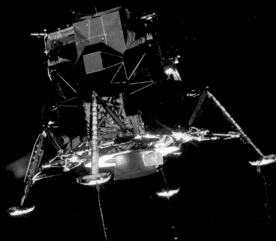

The Apollo 11 Lunar Module, *Eagle*, in descent from *Columbia* to the Moon's surface.

Buzz Aldrin is photographed by Neil Armstrong (visible in Aldrin's visor) standing on the surface of the Moon.

The astronauts' footprints can be seen in the dusty regolith on the Moon's surface.

THE MOON, THE FUTURE

Since 1972, several countries, including Japan and China, have sent unmanned spacecraft to study the Moon. In June 2009, NASA launched the Lunar Reconnaissance Orbiter (LRO) and the Lunar Crater Observation and Sensing Satellite (LCROSS).

LCROSS was made up of a rocket called *Centaur* and a spacecraft that collected data. On October 9, 2009, *Centaur* was crashed into Cabeus, one of the Moon's craters. A cloud of debris from the impact rose nearly 10 miles (16 km) above the crater's rim. Instruments onboard LCROSS and LRO observed and analyzed the material coming from the crater. One of the discoveries was water in the form of ice crystals. This means that permanently shadowed areas of the Moon, such as deep craters, could be a significant source of water.

For decades, scientists have dreamed of building a base on the Moon that could be used as a staging post for missions to other parts of the solar system. The confirmation of water on the Moon, which is an essential resource for human explorers, will bring that dream one step closer.

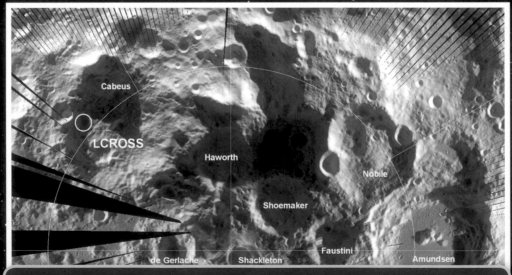

This image of the Moon's South Pole was captured by instruments onboard the LRO. It shows the Cabeus crater (top left) and the position of the LCROSS.

This illustration shows the **LCROSS** spacecraft and *Centaur* separating as they head toward the Moon on October 9, 2009.

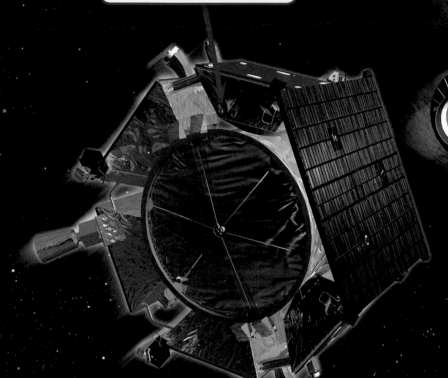

LCROSS spacecraft

Centaur rocket

That's Out of This World!

LCROSS and LRO also found hydrogen gas, ammonia, and methane in the debris cloud from Cabeus. If these gases exist on the Moon in sufficient quantities, it means astronauts living in a lunar base could use them to make fuel. This fuel could be used to run the base, power return trips to Earth, or fuel journeys beyond the Moon.

GLOSSARY

apogee (A-puh-jee)
The point in the Moon's orbit when it is farthest from Earth. When the Moon is at apogee, it is 251,900 miles (405,400 km) away.

asteroids (AS-teh-roydz)
Rocky objects orbiting the Sun and ranging in size from a few feet (m) to hundreds of miles (km) in diameter.

astronauts (AS-truh-nots)
People trained to fly and operate a spacecraft.

astronomer (uh-STRAH-nuh-mer)
A scientist who specializes in the study of outer space.

atmosphere (AT-muh-sfeer)
The layer of gases surrounding a planet, moon, or star.

axis (AK-sus)
An imaginary line about which a body, such as a planet, rotates.

command module
(kuh-MAND MAH-jool) The portion of the Apollo spacecraft that housed the crew, orbited the Moon, and returned the crew to Earth.

cosmonaut (KOZ-muh-naht)
The Russian word for a person who goes into space.

extraterrestrial
(ek-struh-teh-RES-tree-ul)
Outside of the Earth and its atmosphere.

full moon (FUHL MOON)
The phase of the Moon in which its entire disk, or surface facing Earth, is lit by the Sun.

gravity (GRA-vuh-tee)
The force that causes objects to be attracted toward Earth's center or toward other physical bodies in space, such as stars, planets, and moons.

lava (LAH-vuh)
Rock that has been heated within a planet, moon, or asteroid to the point where it flows like a liquid.

lunar module (LOO-ner MAH-jool)
The lander spacecraft in the Apollo program used for traveling between the Moon's surface and another craft orbiting the Moon.

meteoroids (MEE-tee-uh-roydz)
Small particles or fragments that have broken free from an asteroid.

molten (MOHL-ten)
Melted, or liquefied, by heat.

moon (MOON)
A naturally occurring satellite of a planet.

orbits (OR-bits)
The path that an object in space takes as it circles another object.

perigee (PEHR-uh-jee)
The point in the Moon's orbit when it is closest to Earth. When the Moon is at perigee, it is 225,700 miles (363,200 km) away.

planet (PLA-net)
An object in space that is of a certain size and that orbits, or circles, a star.

regolith (REH-guh-lith)
The dusty layer of shattered rock that covers the Moon's surface.

satellite (SA-tih-lyt)
An object that orbits a planet. A satellite may be naturally occurring, such as a moon, or an artificial satellite used for transmitting television or cell phone signals.

solar system (SOH-ler SIS-tem)
The Sun and everything that orbits around it, including planets and their moons, asteroids, meteors, and comets.

Soviet Union
(SOH-vee-et YOON-yun)
A former nation made up of a group of republics in parts of Europe and Asia. The Soviet Union broke up in 1991, creating a group of independent nations, including Russia, Ukraine, Kazakhstan, and Georgia.

universe (YOO-nih-vers)
All of the matter and energy that exists as a whole, including gravity and all the planets, stars, galaxies, and contents of intergalactic space.

WEBSITES

For web resources related to the subject of this book, go to: www.windmillbooks.com/weblinks and select this book's title.

READ MORE

Carlowicz. *The Moon*. New York: Harry N. Abrams, 2008.

Floca, Brian. *Moonshot: The Flight of Apollo 11*. New York: Atheneum, 2009.

Simon, Seymour. *The Moon*. New York: Simon and Schuster Books for Young Readers, 2004.

INDEX